Brown S Gymnast

by Laila Summers
Illustrated by Sonja Bush

SP Sanders
PUBLICATIONS

© 2020 Sanders Publications
All rights reserved.

ISBN 978-1-736354902
Library of Congress Control Number: 2020906605
Illustrated by Sonja Bush

Watch me! Watch me! I can do gymnastics.

First, you have to streeeeetch just like this. I can do a full turn on one foot.

Watch me! Watch me!
I can do a split.

Stand straight up. Slide your legs apart towards the ground. Spread. Spread. Spread as far as you can. Guess what...you did it.

I can do a backbend, a bridge and even a cartwheel.

Watch me! Watch me!
I can do a handstand.

Bend your body toward the ground. Put both hands on the ground. Bring both legs straight up and hold them there. To stay up longer, point your toes. Yes, pointed toes you got it!

Watch me! Watch me!
I can do an elbow stand.

I can do a back roll, a backbend kickover and even a roundoff.

Watch me! Watch me!
I can do a leap split.

Leap forward into the air. Spread your legs apart; just like you would when you do a split. Jump, jump, jump!

Flipping, twisting, turning and jumping is what I like to do. Gymnastics is my favoooorite.

I like to wear my favorite tie dye leotard when I do gymnatics.
What about you?

What can you do?

Can you do a split?
Can you do a bridge?
Can you do a handstand?

Sure you can!
Don't forget...stretch, stretch stretch.
Ready, set, go! On to gymnastics we go.

The End

CPSIA information can be obtained
at www.ICGtesting.com
Printed in the USA
LVHW020838130221
679116LV00011B/1320